I0818548

WNBA

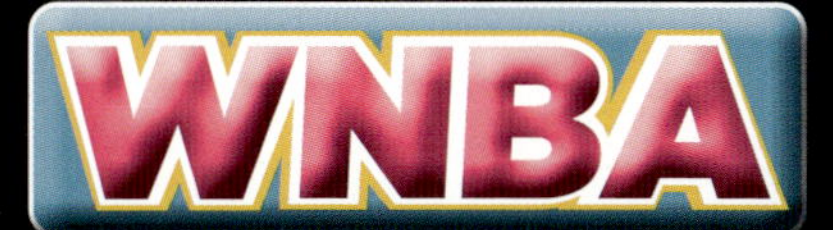

WASHINGTON MYSTICS

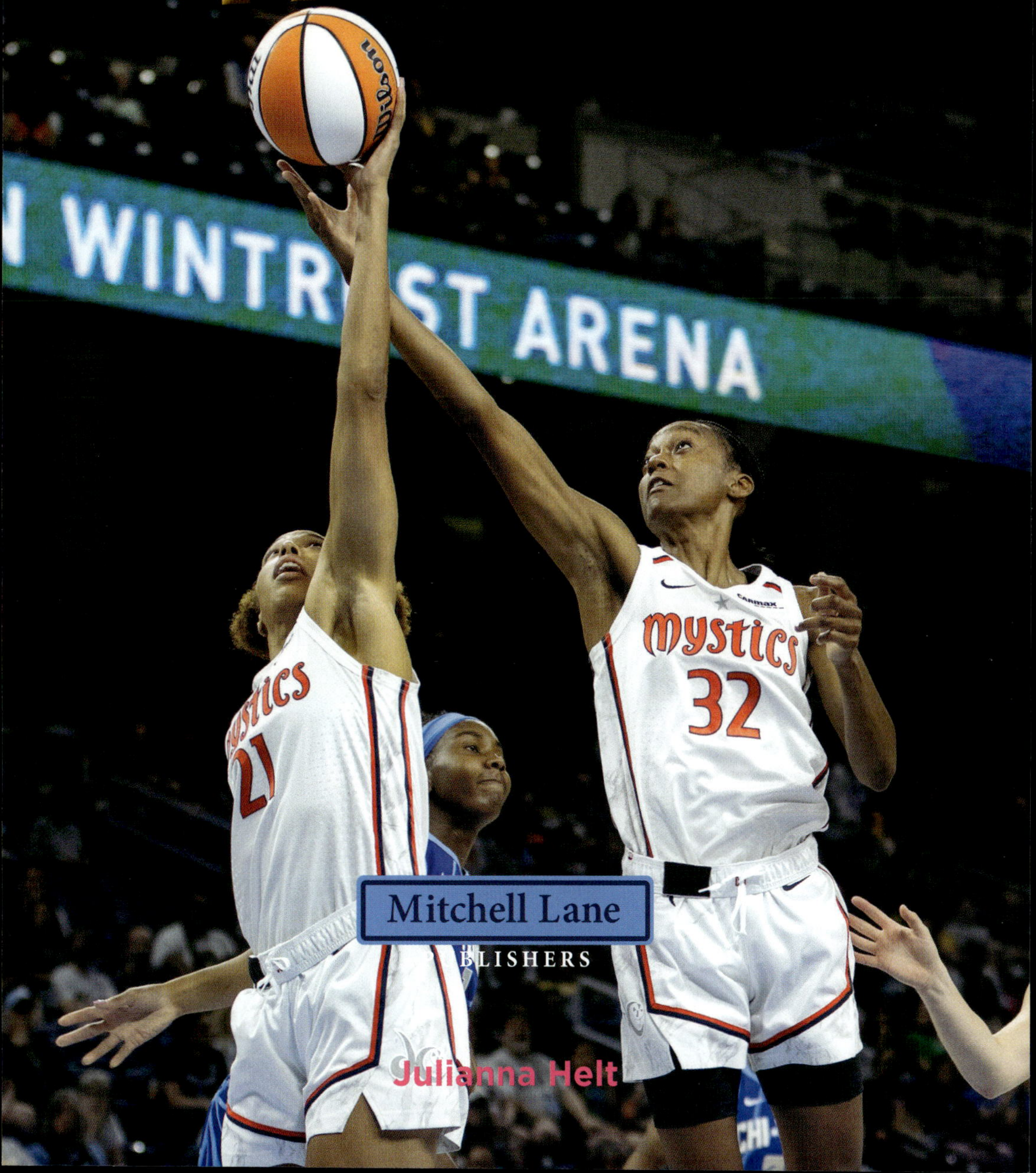

Mitchell Lane
PUBLISHERS

Julianna Helt

Mitchell Lane
PUBLISHERS

mitchelllanepub.com

2001 SW 31st Avenue
Hallandale, FL 33009

First Edition, 2026.
Author: Julianna Helt
Designer: Ed Morgan
Editor: Tammy Gagne

Series: WNBA
Title: Washington Mystics

Library bound ISBN: 979-8-89260-483-3
eBook ISBN: 979-8-89260-486-4

Photo credits: p. 22 sportslogos.net; balance Alamy

CONTENTS

1 The Mystics Win the Championship 4

2 Mystics History 10

3 Mike and Eric Thibault 16

4 Key Mystics Players 22

Glossary 28

Slam Dunk WNBA Trivia 30

Find Out More 31

Index 32

About the Author 32

THE MYSTICS WIN THE CHAMPIONSHIP

Mystics player Natasha Cloud

The Washington Mystics started the 2019 season with one goal: to win a championship. It had never been done in the history of the **franchise**. The team came close the previous year, losing in the finals to the Seattle Storm. But the 2019 season was a historic one for the Washington Mystics.

CHAPTER ONE

The team's players ruled the court from the start with Elena Delle Donne earning the Women's National Basketball Association (WNBA)'s Most Valuable Player (MVP) award. The Mystics finished the season with its best record ever and earned the number one seed in the playoffs. It seemed this was going to be the Mystics' year.

After beating the Las Vegas Aces in the semifinals, Washington was ready to face the Connecticut Sun in the five-game final series. The Mystics and the Sun battled back and forth with each team earning two wins. It all came down to game five. The winner would take all.

Delle Donne was battling a major injury going into the final game. With three **herniated discs** in her back, she would have to dig deep to perform for her team. She told *The New York Times*, "I felt pretty decent today and I also knew today was the last game." Delle Donne went on to score 21 points for her team despite her ailing back.

The Mystics Win the Championship

FAST FACT

Elena Delle Donne has won the WNBA league MVP twice.

Emma Meesseman also showed up for the Mystics, scoring 22 points for the team. Mainly a bench player throughout the season, she became a force in the playoffs. She put up big numbers in both the semifinals and the finals. Her performance earned her the WNBA Finals MVP award. She was the first reserve player in league history to receive the honor.

Delle Donne and Meesseman led the team to an 89–78 victory over the Sun, earning the Mystics that first championship they had set out to claim. Delle Donne said after the win, "It feels **phenomenal**, my goodness, feels so good. Hard to put into words."

The Mystics Win the Championship

Emma Meesseman (right) tries to block a shot in a game against the Connecticut Sun.

Chapter TWO

MYSTICS HISTORY

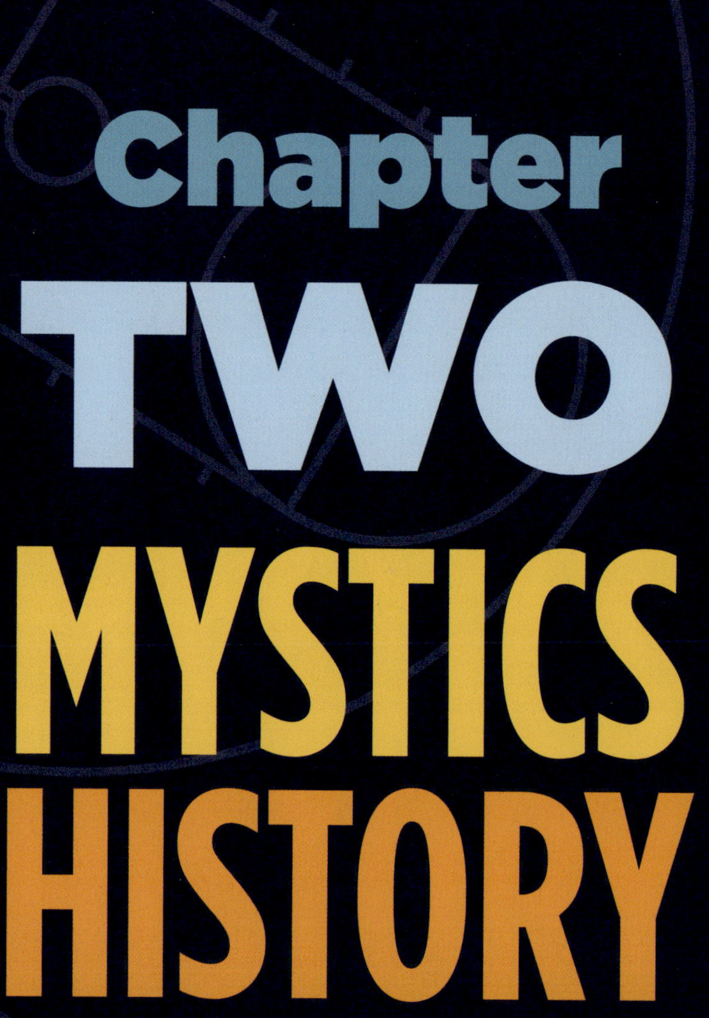

The Mystics' original logo in 1998

The Washington Mystics was created as an **expansion team** in 1998. This was one year after the WNBA was formed. In its first season, the team from Washington, D.C. finished with the worst record in the league. They won just 3 games and lost 27.

CHAPTER TWO

The Mystics received the first draft pick in the 1999 WNBA Draft. They chose University of Tennessee **forward** Chamique Holdsclaw. They improved the next season with Holdsclaw. The team earned its first playoff spot in 2000. In 2002, the Mystics advanced to the Eastern Conference Finals. But they lost to the New York Liberty.

In 2005, the team was sold to a group that included Sheila C. Johnson, making her the first Black woman to own a WNBA team. The sale also made her the first woman to be an owner of three professional sports teams. Johnson told *The Seattle Times*, "I hope that this is a signal that it's about time that a woman, and an African American woman, is part of this whole scene of sports."

Mystics History

When Sheila C. Johnson became a Mystics owner, she also held ownership in the Washington Wizards and the Washington Capitals.

CHAPTER TWO

The team returned to the playoffs in 2009 and 2010 with forward Crystal Langhorne. In 2012, Mike Thibault was hired as head coach. He led the team to six playoff appearances and their first WNBA championship.

Joining the Mystics in 2019, Kristi Toliver was **instrumental** in bringing the championship title to Washington, D.C. that year. She served as both a player and an assistant coach of the team. After winning the final game, Toliver told *The New York Times*, "All I said to the team before the game was, 'Regret nothing.'" And the Mystics did just that. Toliver scored 18 points in the game five win over the Connecticut Sun.

Mystics History

Kristi Toliver is a strong player who has also helped coach the Mystics.

FAST FACT

The Mystics play their home games at the Entertainment & Sports Arena in Washington, D.C.

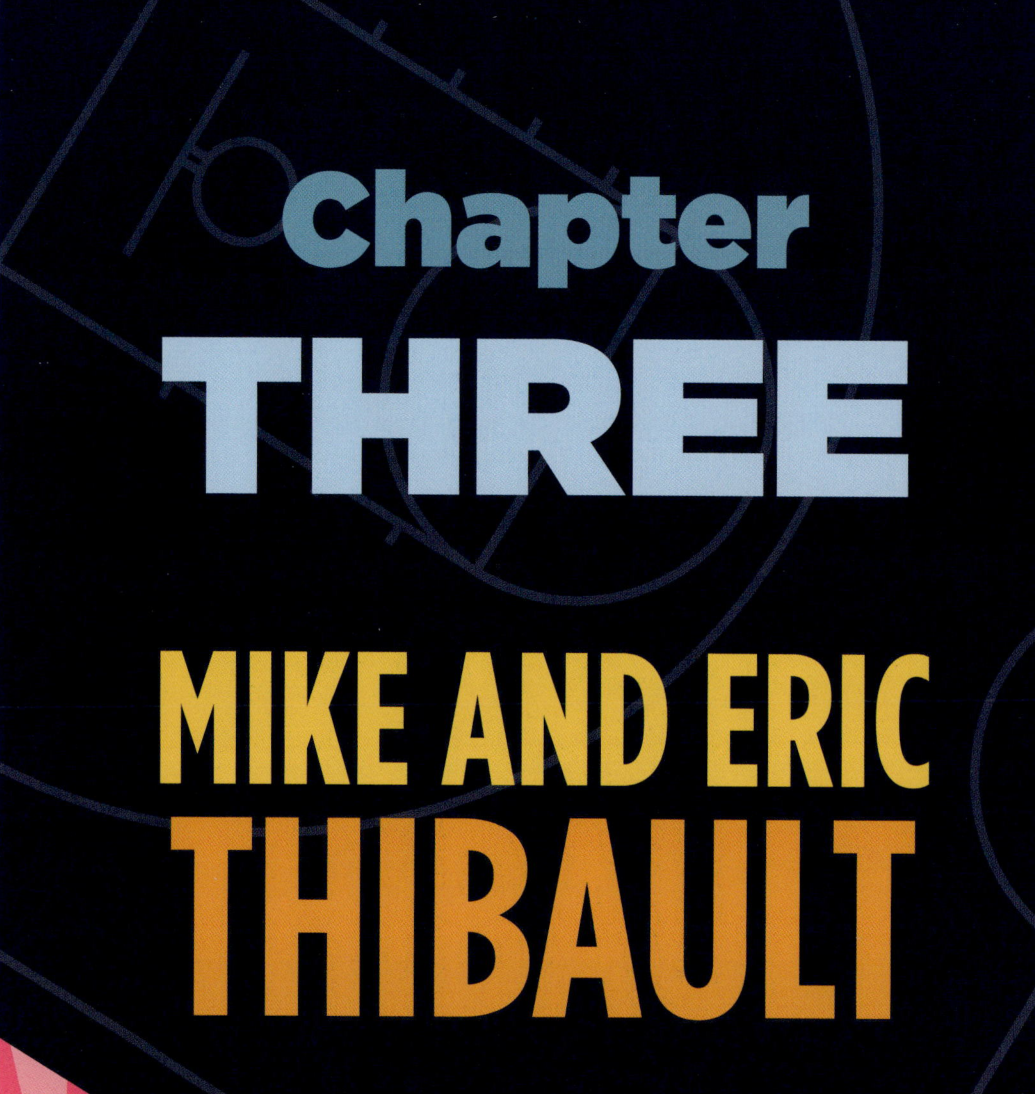

Chapter THREE

MIKE AND ERIC THIBAULT

Mike Thibault

Mike Thibault was named the WNBA Coach of the Year after his first season with the Mystics. This was his third time winning the award. Over the next seven seasons, the Mystics missed the playoffs just once, in 2016.

CHAPTER THREE

Thibault was responsible for bringing Elena Delle Donne to the team in 2017. At 6 feet, 5 inches (1.9 m) tall, she had become a standout player with the Chicago Sky. He believed Delle Donne's height, skills, and leadership were exactly what the Mystics needed to reach the championship level.

On June 17, 2021, Thibault recorded his 350th career win in a game against the Atlanta Dream. The next year, he announced his retirement. By this time, he had led the Mystics to eight postseason appearances and one championship. He ended his career as the winningest coach in WNBA history with a record of 379–289.

Mike and Eric Thibault

Elena Delle Donne hugs head coach Mike Thibault.

CHAPTER THREE

Ted Leonsis is the chief executive officer (CEO) of Monumental Sports & Entertainment. This is the organization that owns the Washington Mystics. Upon Thibault's retirement, Leonsis said, "When we first hired Mike ten years ago, we assigned him a large task: to make the Washington Mystics **relevant** in the WNBA, and he more than delivered."

Mike's son, Eric Thibault, took over as head coach for the team in 2023. He served in this role until the end of 2024 when Sydney Johnson was selected as the team's new head coach. He was the assistant coach under his father for ten years. The younger Thibault helped get the team to all eight of its postseason appearances, including the 2019 championship.

After taking the head coaching job, Eric told *Sportskeeda*, "I'm ready to help the Mystics get back to the championship level that our fans, players, and staff expect." In his first season as head coach, the Mystics made it to the playoffs but lost in the first round to the New York Liberty.

Mike and Eric Thibault

Eric Thibault (left), Mike Thibault (center), and assistant coach Marianne Stanley (right)

FAST FACT

Mike and Eric Thibault are the only father and son who have both coached in the WNBA.

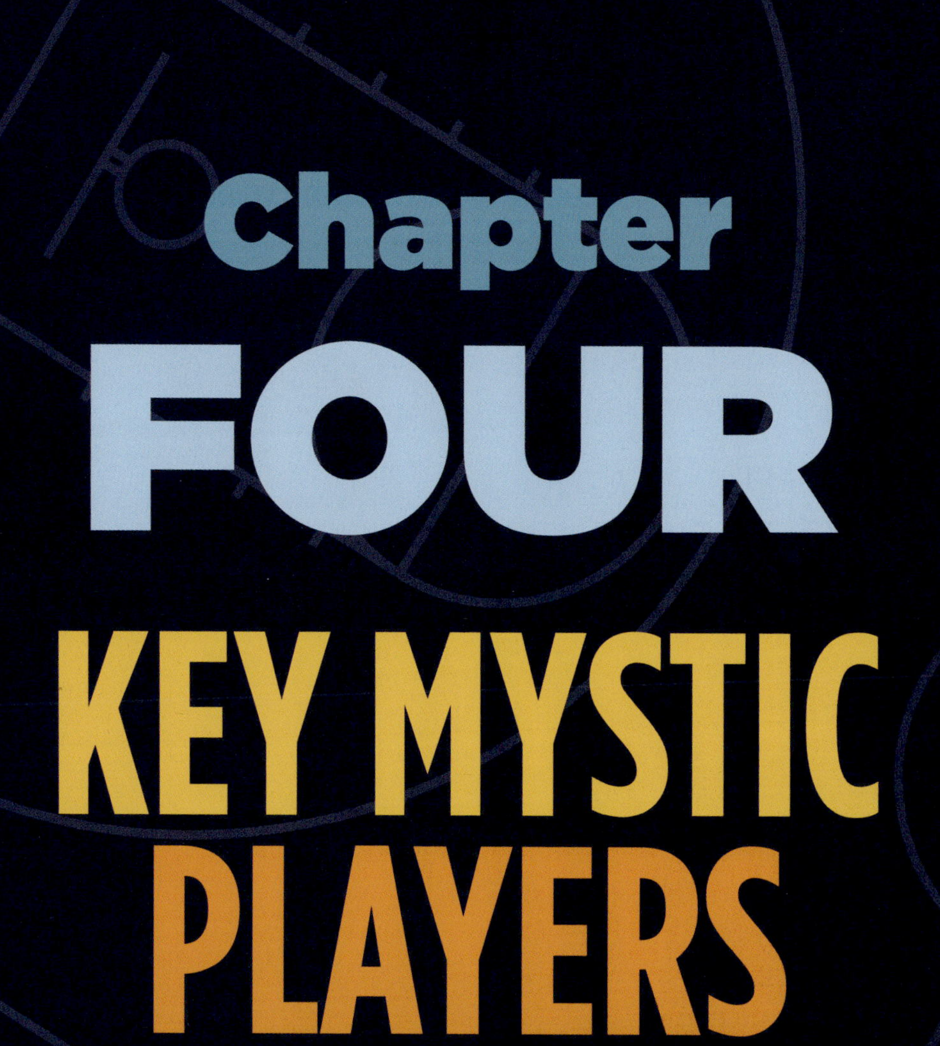

Chapter FOUR

KEY MYSTIC PLAYERS

Ariel Atkins (left) and Shakira Austin (right)

Two players who have made the biggest **impact** on the Washington Mystics team are Ariel Atkins and Shakira Austin. Atkins was selected by the Washington Mystics in the 2018 WNBA Draft. Mike Thibault shared his thoughts about this new player with the *Laredo Morning Times*. "I think that her basketball **IQ** and energy level is off the charts," he said.

CHAPTER FOUR

Atkins was in her second year with the team when they won the 2019 WNBA Championship. She also made the WNBA All-Defensive second team for the second time. This honor recognizes the top defensive players in the league each year. She would go on to become the first player in WNBA history to make an All-Defensive team in each of her first five seasons in the league.

A two-time WNBA All-Star, Atkins kept getting better. In the 2024 season, she scored a career-high 36 points in single game for the Mystics. This would tie the franchise record for the second-most points in a game. Elena Delle Donne holds both the first spot with 37 points and the shared second spot with Atkins. Washington traded Atkins to the Sky ahead of the 2025 season.

Key Mystic Players

FAST FACT

Alana Beard is the franchise leader for points scored, with 3,128 in her career.

CHAPTER FOUR

The future of the Mystics looks bright. Young stars, such as Shakira Austin, are making big names for themselves. Austin was drafted in the first round of the 2022 WNBA Draft. She was named to the All-**Rookie** WNBA team that year.

After having back surgery in the offseason, Austin returned in the 2024 season. She was ready to continue helping the Mystics move forward. During her first game upon her return, she had a career-high 5 blocks. Ariel Atkins talked about Austin after the game. "I see her growing every time I see her on the floor," she told reporters.

The Mystics worked their way from the bottom of the WNBA in their first year to the top of the league in 2019. They have come close to a repeat several times. With both seasoned **veterans** and young talent, the Washington Mystics are ready to repeat their 2019 championship season.

Key Mystic Players

Shakira Austin jumps to make a shot in a game against the Chicago Sky.

GLOSSARY

expansion team
A new team that is added to an existing league

forward
A basketball player who plays near the basket, often rebounding and scoring points

franchise
A team in a professional sport league

herniated discs
Rubbery cushions between the bones in the spine that have been forced out of place

IQ
A slang term for knowledge about a particular subject

impact
A strong effect on someone or something

instrumental
Playing an important role in an accomplishment

phenomenal
Remarkable or extraordinary

relevant
Important to the current time or situation

rookie
An athlete playing her first season as a member of a professional sports team

veterans
Players with extensive experience

SLAM DUNK WNBA TRIVIA

- The Washington Mystics' name was chosen to go along with the name of the Washington Wizards, which is their National Basketball Association (NBA) counterpart.
- The Mystics team colors are red, navy blue, silver, and white.
- The Mystics team sponsor is the GEICO insurance company.
- The Washington Mystics' mascot is Pax the Panda. He is said to have been born at the Smithsonian National Zoo in Washington, D.C.
- Chamique Holdsclaw holds the Mystics record for most rebounds in a single game, with 24.
- A skilled free-throw shooter, Elena Delle Donne holds the record for the highest free-throw percentage in WNBA history, at 93.4 percent.

FIND OUT MORE

IN PRINT

Coffelt, Nancy. *Connecticut Sun*. Mitchell Lane Publishers, 2026.

Davidson, B. Keith. *WNBA*. Crabtree Publishing, 2022.

O'Neal, Ciara. *The WNBA Finals*. Apex, 2023.

ON THE INTERNET

Washington Mystics.
https://mystics.wnba.com.

"Washington Mystics," *ESPN*, n.d.
www.espn.com/wnba/team/_/name/wsh/washington-mystics.

"Washington Mystics," *FOX Sports*, n.d.
www.foxsports.com/wnba/washington-mystics-team.

INDEX

Atkins, Ariel, 23–24, 26
Atlanta Dream, 18
Austin, Shakira, 23, 26
awards, 6, 8, 17
Chicago Sky, 18
Connecticut Sun, 6, 8, 14
Delle Donne, Elena, 6, 7, 8, 18, 24, 30
founding, 11
Holdsclaw, Chamique, 12, 30
Johnson, Sheila C., 12
Langhorne, Crystal, 14
Las Vegas Aces, 6
Meesseman, Emma, 8
New York Liberty, 12, 20
records, 6, 11, 18, 20, 24, 30
Seattle Storm, 5
Thibault, Eric, 20, 21
Thibault, Mike, 14, 17, 18, 20, 21, 23
Toliver, Kristi, 14

About the Author

Julianna Helt is a children's-librarian-turned-author. She enjoys researching and writing about all sorts of topics, including women in sports. Her favorite WNBA player is Caitlin Clark. When Julianna isn't writing, she enjoys reading and solving puzzles. She lives with her family in Pittsburgh, Pennsylvania.